Cupid's Dark Diary

Acts of Greed, Lust, and Obsession

WE DoMore

Copyright © 2024 WE DoMore
All rights reserved
First Edition

Fulton Books
Meadville, PA

Published by Fulton Books 2024

ISBN 979-8-89427-249-8 (paperback)
ISBN 979-8-89427-250-4 (digital)

Printed in the United States of America

The Key

So you want me? No, you need me; it's a must that you have me. How long can you wait to obtain me? How long can you go without me? You can't, and you'd happily say it just to have me. The touch, the feel—just the thought of me being next to you—makes you hotter than the last time I hurt you. Sweet tears full of love, hate, and pain. All the things needed to grow; sunshine and rain. So you wait for me and give me time to grow, like maybe only time will show.

The first time I saw you, I knew you. I knew it was you by the way you talked to me. You opened me up in a seemingly easy way. Over food and wine, you give me, please. With no thought of where this night might end, we close the space that stands between us. With smiles and grinds, you welcome me in. Chest to chest and the feel of this breath. There is no need to rush to the end, but we both know we must go all in. This is not just another; this is you. The one I've waited for and wanted. It's here at last, and how we wish it would last.

I'm here for you, and I'm sorry for you. Like a rose held without thought of the thorns, you find yourself bleeding. I love that you keep trying. Taking the good with the bad and mixing it up for happier days. Where you get the gains from those pains, this feeling will always last. Fade and brighten, but never darken. We shine bright in our romance, have fallen deep in this love, and are fulfilled with even greater lust.

Tweist

Hey there, lovely lady. I've been waiting and wanting.
I've been watching and learning.
It's my turn, and I won't waste this time.
See, I know how you like to grind.
The truth behind those eyes.
She darty, darty, darty wine.
All while she's on fire between those thighs.
Hoping I make her feel like a kid again.
Zaddy's gonna put me on his knee again.
Cry, babe, cry.
There she went, running again.
Always calling me the lie.
Sorry babe I'm just a guy.
Don't get mad and call me the other guy.
I just chased the tail to bury the bone.
I never said I was in need of a home.

I Like, I Want

I see you more like me as the minutes pass. You wait for me to see you as my equal while I wait to see you equally. The pain I cause is not even understanding how deep the love you have for me goes. So you wait, like having a baby. I don't want to lie; I honestly try. Over and over with the same lie, like I'm getting better. It takes time; I can't change overnight. Why can't you just see I'm trying, and I have gotten better? We all slip from time to time. I admit I slip more than others; I'm just asking for time. Can't you see that I'm here? I want to be here, and here is where I always find myself.

There's nothing like being here with you. It can be so amazing the way you pull me in. It's like you're saving me. You are a light bringer because you brought light to my dark and lonely world. How could I hurt you this way when my intentions were good? How I wish I could take this pain away until the day you share the same pain with me. It is brokenhearted, all I give over and over with no stop on this repeat.

I wish I could have gotten it then. All the lonely nights while you lay next to me, to yourself. You must have felt, LORD, how can this be? It almost seems as if this must be a stranger sleeping with me. I look away, and you make sure I see you crying to be with me. You see, it's true that you feed me what I kill and bring to you. Did I really give you the love I killed, and in kind, you gave me dead love? A hard meal was then prepared over time through lonely, sad, and crying nights. I get that this is why I just can't eat, drink, or sleep. I'm catching it in repeat, the way I was and how I should have been, and I'll soon learn the ways of treating a GIFT.

She Do What She Wants

First off, we ain't saying she ain't classy.
We just know she likes to get a li'l nasty.
No need to dress it up, it's fine with me.
Shit, let her gonna and do that dance.
All I see is that she nasty like me.
See, she is classy and alright with me.
Did you know she was even into bragging.
Like, he was lying if he said he hit me.
She wit it like, spilled tea, who really got rode this week.
Stop hating; she a champ in these streets.
Bold, Beautiful, and tasteful, know she a treat.
Never the trick, like ain't gone be none of that pass shit.
She really rolling with the click,
Don't worry, li'l sis got her own nine.
That Gucci holds her extended clips.
Just en case any want to trip.
She be like, I'm bi trick,
I hit tops and bottoms with this bitch.

Blinded Heart

He doesn't see it. How could he possibly get it? Yet it's staring him right in the face. As he lets the minutes turn into hours and the days into nights. You are a strong woman. Yes, tough indeed. You love a man who is only a man. What a fool he is to not see the love you have given him. And yet time and again, you, yes, you woman, want to be by his bedside. While you wait to love him and want to know him. This strange game we play to pass the time. I, too, wonder when the rules change. Is it a debate or a chase? This game is mine, and it is more dangerous than Russian Roulette. Hearts bleed, and words are broken. But strong women play the best. They simply wait, and as time passes, what he cannot see, he sees when there is no time left to wait. You strong woman will grow stronger while you wait. The day comes when you no longer see what you saw in the man and can no longer wait for it to be received. Yes, a stronger woman after the wait, well prepared to leave and live. To see what her life is like. When she sees and learns to see her, she's not blinded by her heart, in need of just a man who can only lie about what she can't see. Leading her astra when she can't see; some men are not yet men. They themselves can't see, and they never learn to wait; they only want. To want the woman of dreams. A picture that keeps a man blinded to the words that God has given to the woman. The ability to wait on the right man.

Reaching

Am I reaching? I might be. This feeling got me feeling high, and I can see us reaching new heights. So I will keep on reaching out and waiting for you to take my hand. Like, you're ready to go. We roll out like dows, leaving a trail; there is no need to ask where we go. They already know. I'm her teacher, not her preacher. When she starts reaching, I'm the one breaching. Time and time she reaches climax; that's her limit, and for the door she goes. I could be reaching, but every time I reached, I stopped her from walking out the door. Leave me thinking: did I really reach her? The words I spoke, the ways I touched her body, and the way I held her in my arms. Will it really have her reach to hold me when she lays down to sleep? Is it reaching to think that I've made it? When you're reaching for me while I'm reaching for you, I'm reaching your dreams with the words I've spoken to you. Not to wet your thighs, but to be stuck in her mind on rewind. You can call it a game, but there'll be no fuel when I'm there. This is patience; I know how to wait and take my time. I learned you like school days. Tell them to stop reaching out and saying I'm bad for you, because I don't want to be finished with you, like dropouts do. In time, the panties drop too. Tell me, then, I just want to be beside you and take a look inside and see what's real. Is it fine that I want to reach out to the real you? See, I know we've all cried and been down. I'm not trying to get you mad; it's just that I want to know your past. I know it's not all good, but I'm reaching to see what made you look this good. Reaching deeper and deeper inside, learning what makes you, you, brings me closer. Is it reaching to say I'm reaching for your soul, all of you, when you lay in my bed? Looking at, say to me, how much closer can I really get?

Anna

It's sad to say we're just friends—no, really friends. Without a doubt, I love her, but I'm not her lover. She belongs to another, and still after that brother, another brother. I have been watching this shit for too long. Listen to you play me like a brother, telling me everything I need to be your perfect lover. But again and again, you tell me your heart is with this new brother. Why do I play? Wait and see how this plays out. Over and over, we still cry together. She cherishes this when she can't see how we can be friends and lovers. So I try to hold on and still love her while I know she's with someone else. Maybe with just another season, she could see what I could be; it makes me wonder. Should I leave and be with someone else. But still, I wait, playing amazed when it doesn't have wedding bells with another.

Sky

So fly she is; you can't lie. Other girls try to
match her fly. Nice try, little fly.
Look at her; she knows flies can fly, but
not to the sky, although they try.
She doesn't smoke, and her fly still tops the high.
Keep buying plane tickets just to get in the sky.
The view is amazing; this scenery, I know
only the good lord made it.
Now lay me down to sleep. Lord, let me
grow wings so I can touch the sky.
Wow, it's a bird; it's a plane; no, it's her; got
every man wanting to save her.
She doesn't need to be saved, Wonder Woman in disguise.
Like a good mama and papa raised her.
She can cook the meals, change the oil, and handle the kids.
Looking at the sky like that sounds like a keeper, not to
mention she has a bag and knows how to keep it.
With her, the sky's the limit; she knows her worth, and
like a rocket ship, she'll take you out of this world.

Don't Do Too Much

Cool. She likes you, but don't do too much. Don't break the rules, acting like a fool. Baby, I need you. Boy, you need too much. She wants to be hold down, not held down. Always trying to be huge and emotional with a bitch. *"Pause; ladies, I use this word the way you ladies have told me. It's only for your enjoyment. Please in enjoy."* Again, with doing too much. Stay in your lane, the one you built for. Get it, got it, not good; she wants to be chased, not put in first place. You; winning is good.

Second half,

Act like a sportsmen

Get back on defense, and try to keep your eyes on the ball. Oh, she likes baseball. Balls and bats, Goo Kats. Runner on second, can you hear the Kat saying steal third? Now you've bout got it. Always play it cool as if it's the bottom of the ninth, her bases are full, and you're up to bat with no outs. A hit to win a home run to make her happy. The ladies say amen. Now they got it, good. Take the bat and hit it good. Out of the park, what a way to end the show!

Marry

This is a tale unlike any fairy tale. For the girl here was once white as snow. Whom they all called a dream girl.

No, Marry was a real dream girl, lost in her own world. With thoughts of love and marriage. Lost in her thoughts, as the lamb led to slaughter. Deeper and deeper, she falls in love. Finding a bottom with no marriage to land.

You should know Marry could never give up hope. She finds her footing over and over again. The way only a woman could. Soon she'll be back at it again. Jumping off the cliff of love, only to find an empty bottom.

Scared from head to toe from dreaming of love. This once ray of sunshine has closed herself off from love. Like the princess in the tower. She knows she cannot give up on love.

So there, Marry waits. For the day, the knight can slay her dragon of fairness. Scale her wall to her heart and enhance her with love and marriage.

Laly

Let's turn the page to a lady who's making her own way in the world. She's not starred-eyed, and the girl can't afford to be dazed.

She got to stick and move, stick and move; after every little hit, she got out of dodge.

Right, go left, step back, and fix your stands. This girl's a beast, and they think you're playing; show 'em how you really dance.

Footwork, footwork on to the next, once she gets you up against the ropes. Every time, they keep going down. Give her the belt, she'll take a ring too, but she's not looking for marriage. She is not with no hours or carriage.

She talks about her cabbage, lettuce, and blue cheese, even though, but no, she's no oh.

Lady, one of those with it from head to toe, is hard to get, harder to keep, and impossible to forget. Yeah, that's it. Knock out bad.

She is not playing with sticks; her pitch is lit. She's easy to forget a hit, like it's play to win, not to the end.

Act I

Keep playing like a baller, and you're gonna be the lonely one. Keep playing like you're shooting in the gym, and you're gonna need another door to walk in. You keep playing like a star and miss out on your biggest fan. No, keep playing, she's not your ma'am, so she wants to stop your fun. Keep playing with those who can't help you get something, you should know you're going to end up with none. Don't look this way, don't look that way. After all that playing, she started acting like you ain't worth none. When she's gone, she's gone; ain't no playback. Now you're playing old love songs, but she doesn't want to hear that. Truly, she wishes she could get her WAP back, so she'll take half your stacks and still be mad. No, not at you with your playing ass. With her always acting like it was all cool ass. Seeing how she feels doesn't feel good to men. But being home is the only lonely one. When she got friends, you can both see how it all came to an end.

Low

Low like get on down, but she up tho
Low like burn 'em down, but she rolls 'em up tho
Low like hold me down; she like 'em stand up
Low like go down, she know how to get it up
Low like lay down, she watch 'em stand up
Low likes to put it down; she makes 'em can't stand up
Low stays down; her man holds her up
Low like they don't know, but everybody up on it tho
Low like it ain't for show, but still ain't trying to hide it
Low like I'm counting my dough, why they trying to count it tho
Low like stay down to earth, but out of
this world like stars up in the sky
Low like take a knee, she's an angel from above.

His

It's said that with age comes wisdom, and it's sad to see what you thought isn't quite so. How hard can these life lessons be? You live and you learn, right? Not so right, if you go through the same lesson twice.

It seems as if we can't get the message or lesson. Try as we might to do right; it can't seem to be seen what's right. Asking questions like what do you like trying to get it right.

Could it be the time, or maybe my mind? Playing it back in rewind should have gifted more time. My ways of love weren't your thoughts. Was it romancing your heart was lacking; being patient, forever waiting for me to stop thinking money and just give you time.

Open my mind and open your heart when given full attention. I won't give up on the lesson; I'm built for the testing. With more focus, I will open your heart. With more time, I will enter your heart. I open and grow, entering and finally touching your heart, soul, and mind.

Her's

Stooop…What are you doing to me? Noo stooop…I ain't never felt like this. Why do you keep looking at me? No, it's like you're touching me. I can feel you all in me.

I'm weak; hooow, you open me. Take your time with me, like you are not trying to draw please from me. The way you move is more through me. Yes, I can really feel you in me.

This is safe, the way you hold me. I am fully open to pulling you; let's get closer. Forgetting I'm me, I feel you forgetting you're you. This is it, the one I seek and want; opened up and fully flowing, I'm free to go weak.

Harriet

Nana we are not talking, run away. But this one is something like a runaway. More times than Harriet, she runs away. She likes the fun and enjoys getting some. But open to none. Like Harriet, who is looking for a master, she's gonna set herself free. Call her Harriet; she runs from weak love. She wants to get caught by none, so she shakes the scent. Make him crawl through the mud and miss you on the other side. While you make you way north and then back south, to him, that makes you feel right. After waiting all night for the light, the coast is clear. To freedom, she goes to him who can open her and fill her with his fullness, moving ever more and more through her. The breath of freedom to let be. This is why she ran away, to run for the freedom she feels with him. Strong yet soft, warrior yet safe, King yet servant, and he praises the goddess in you. How you love to run to him, and find he's in loving graces. This is why she ran away to be free in her love, knowing he could stand her love. She freely opens with no force from him, welcoming the full gift of him. He is truly free, making it so Harriet doesn't have to run any more.

S'um Like a Song

Every time I go for a walk, I get these jazzy tones going through my head. There we go, like "It's All in My Head" and "I'd Rather Be with You." Like I can hear her life's soundtrack. "I'm Sorry Miss Jackson," "Killing Me Softly," and "Single Ladies." Why I see deep when I walk down the street, "Just My Imagination." Yeah, the beauty is more than skin deep, but I know "Girls Just Want to Have Fun, Anaconda," and "FNF (Let's Go)." This beauty is Poison. Yeah, I like the oldies, but I got "Time Today," and she showed me how she "Scrub the Ground". Okay, okay, can you see how it's hard to walk uptown funk, got me like "Adorn," "I Get Around." But it all seems to go by slowly; even when I'm driving, it's like I'm walking, and beautiful things go by like flowers and butterflies; the sight of you, "My Girl." Seeing you walk away, "I Wish It Would Rain." The beauty GOD gifted me to see, has some like I'm starry-eyed talking like I can see the sunshine in between the rain. "Keep Ya Head Up," think above the sky, and see "Brighter Days." This feelin' I get when walking is soul reaching like "Lean on Me," not lust felled it's GOD In Me, I Smile. I see the women of the world, and I see the beauty that GOD gifted me to see, and I love what I see. When I walk, it's like I'm walking with you.

Once

Just once is all I need, like one hope and one dream. Let me take my time just once. Line the shot up right. Just once I'm playing to win, I leave it all on the field. Just once I'm going all in to the end, I want to leave no doubt to think about. Just once, it's my time, and if not, call it fraud. Just once I want to fake it, I'll leave what you see to you. Just once, I love it fully and still stay focused on my business. Just once, ready or not, I'm taking a chance; it takes guts to win. Just once I look past my fear and tell the truth, I begin to win. Just once tell me your way, if I listen can I win. Just once, I'll do it your way; no one else has lost. Just once, I didn't have to find you; this love was never lost. Just once I have a dream, you say no vision; now create. Just once, I meant the words I say: You show yourself to stay. Just once is all I have to give, and over and over I give it fully. Just once is all that can be given; with no man the owner of time and only in the mind can we rewind. Just once I'm decisive with this choice, there is no time to wait or delay; it's in play with no pause today. Once is what I got, and once is a chance of a lifetime. Once is now, always love how it looks. Once it is prefect it doesn't change or stay the same. Once, just once, I give over to time and enjoy this presence fully with love.

So'so

No pressure; calm down; you can wait. Remember, you have time today. That doesn't mean don't go; you can just go slow. Always go; just choose how you want to go. Somebody says slow and steady. Yeah, you can win the race; just know when to pick up the pace. No jerk I'm Jake, yes, Sir Tradesman. Modern day exchange man plays with more than one plan, good with both hands. Something like a Goodman looks good with the shirt tucked and raised when the lady stands. Something like a bad boy, don't take your shirt off. How I make her heart hurt? It's clear I'm keen to pen and pad that's how I get the point. Am I the player? I'm not trying to score a point. What's my objective? We don't precisely see the same side of me. Is there two sides to me? You can tell me. If I touch your mind and you give me your body and your soul, I'm sure to find it. How could I play with your mind? Have you really given over to me, or do you want to play with my mind? Straight line you beside me; I can't see how I see, though you know where I've planned to go. Don't trust me; see me missing nothing. Why lie when honest men keep their gains. Don't let my truth hurt, because it's not my truth; it's yours. I know we try, but what I see, I see, so no one other than me can see. Even when you look, you can't see how far I've come so far. What I see can't be told; you have to feel it and open up to let it fall on you. I have no fear of running out of gas, like the racer I make my way past. Look at me go!

HR

Yeah. You know better, and don't tell me that I couldn't help myself. We can see you can't help yourself; that's why you're sitting here. So we can see if I can help; why don't you tell me when you feel the problem began?

Well, I don't have a problem, nor do I see the problem. If it's a problem, it's not my problem. I recommend for me not to be mixed in it; see problem solving is my business, and I can put an end to it.

So you have nothing in it; just what he says, she says. It's the world at play; I get it; they just can't see it your way. They never really try it your way, it's always their way or no way. It must be hard; when all you do is be calm and do it their way.

Yeah, and no. I'm not lying; it's just that most of it just feels like it's for show. Like the growth, is this helping or hurting? Just what is there to show, it can't be only hope. Is it even known where we're going, or could it be that it's cool if we land where we land?

So you can't live life without a plan, and there should be some demands. You seem to have something in mind, pardon me if I'm stepping over any lines. Could hope be a kin to a single bar soap, like coming to the end of your rope. You're not trying to go that far, but it's clear you're tired of being broke.

So is there hope that broken thing can be fixed?

To fix what's broken, it takes work. Are you willing to do the work?

How So

Different—what is that? Is it the same for me as for you? What are you seeing to make you think that? You aren't me, are you? If not, why would you think that? You think about what you say, like what to say or how to play. I should never admit to seeing; either way, you'll say, "Can't you see?" Indeed, I say not, unless you want to know why. That difference I can't explain, and dear, do not try to play the fool. Then what could I say? I'm sorry, I'm truly a fool. All words seem to fail me, for I know not which you hear of the words I speak. I know not this difference between yours and ours. Tell me what you see, even though I fear to ask. Is it truly like to what you hear? If not, then is it what you're hearing that's a mistake, or could what you're seeing be an illusion of what you're thinking? Like when you say different, to who or to what. How are you viewing me? Is it like me? I just can't see, not through the eyes you see. No, I'm not blind, but still, I dear not to say I can see. Tell me, when you say you can see, what is it that you see. Is it me, like light or matter, not just a reflection of how you see? How So is it different? I can't say I see, seeing that there's light in you and me that can be truly bright. You see, I seek enlightenment so the light might burn bright once I truly know thee.

David

Me being me I know all too well when it comes to man, and no, not mankind, just man. I mean, it is his world. Yes, oh yes, we know it's his world, but it would be much of nothing if it weren't for you, lovely women. But could it be somewhere that someone was deceived at some point and the rest just followed the lead? How so indeed, but if not, why do these hearts here bleed? Should I, dear, say it's too much that's wanted from man? To the point where just he can't be with one woman. Why can't he just be with you? He's a man after GOD's own heart. So he should be able to love just me and only me, you say. Then what of GOD and the love that's gifted to man? You say to be a good man, but do you not know some of GOD's men. First, it was once said to lead by example; thus David, a man after GOD's own heart, was said to have just how many wives. You object, OKAY, this man of GOD took another's wife, then had him killed. Following which, he's still a man after GOD's own heart. Still, it's not right, but it must go on, for who are we to kill the dream, hope, or soul of another.

Act II

Always the bride's maid, never the bride. Be true to what man you see yourself catering to. That sounds like being a maid to you— what she says she do. That's too much for you, and you want to marry who? Who am I to say if there's somebody for everybody? Think about it: What's that man like you wanting from GOD? How you think he is going about his life must be nice, right? He came full, so what can you do to be his Mrs. Right. Think twice: no man is right, and none could be that nice. Only if they are not leaving life do few enjoy that kind of life. Truly, who doesn't like the bright lights and the nightlife? But it hurt once, twice, thrice, maybe you should look in the daylight. Say again what you're waiting for; no, I'm not raining down on you. But by the count, it's raining men, and you don't like how people live their lives. Let's think dog; all men are right. If you say so, then why would you think to find a good man? It's OKAY. You, be the best you, the good thing, and let the right man find you. You're made to stand the test; give that man your best. Show that love you hold to the vest and what it brings out the best. That bad boy grows with love into that good man. You can't rush the man; just watch for love in the man. Test their belief that only time can tell and that they are the only thing to heal all wombs.

Tracie

Well, let's call her Tracie. Yeah she s'um like a racer. She doesn't have patience and doesn't believe in waiting. She knows how to get you on all ten toes and make you feel like you're chasing. Ain't it breathtaking? Go ahead and call her captivating. But this sight can't last when she passes and passes. It seems as if every man is bound to crash; she gives none a pass. Don't make her laugh; she doesn't need you to last. With roses, she brightens up; you should know how to make it last. Play like a racer and watch her get past fast. Can't spectate and wait for a crash; they get into the chase when they like to race. Hug the curve and stay on her tail. She is going to try and shake you, maybe even bait you. Be patient, hold your lane, and get in her wind stream. You want the win; she's no rookie. She'll make you put it all in, whether you're big or headed home. Show any hesitation, like you can't grip the wheel; it's dust you're smoking, so you just can't win. Is she a really good racer or a danger? Call it a win; she didn't have to wait to the end. Trying to take her, they never had an in; every one of them, Tracie, was their end. Last man standing, she says how, when, and which one can withstand it. Tracie.

MIA

Listen, my friend gives me a call.
No, not exactly exciting.
To they start sounding like they mint to call the police.
You with me things going to heat up fast…
Now this friend isn't someone I say is chill.
Cool, yeah. Chill no.
Hints why they sound like they need 9-1-1

It really happened.

What's going on you, alright?
How it usually goes

I can't find them; I've looked everywhere.
I don't know what is going on.
I don't know what to do.

Who is them, what's going on? Talk to me.
Sounds like you feelin' it and really being put through it.

No, this could really be it.
I don't even know what happened.
One minute there they were, then the next gone.
Why me? How can this be? I should have seen something like this
    could happen.

Take a breath and let it out.
Help is here; just say what you need.

They didn't really leave, and if so then, where they ever really here.
Take your time, slow and steady.
No pain, no gain; you got to work through it, not work it out.
So have you heard anything back yet.

They just walked in.

Nicole

She knows what she's 'bout. So to you, she seems cold, but her heart ain't frozen. Man, she is full of gold. Yeah, her name is Nicole; Mama made her out of gold. She can handle any weather and stand against the cold. She will be getting dollars, making the brothers want to holler. Send 'em back to their mama; get them boys proper. Getting checks all weather, she doesn't understand the pressure. You can't feel the pressure when it's gold and diamonds. Claiming up the ladder, get letters; she can't stop the shining; you're going to have to wait for her to decline. Forced on her mission like shots and ladders. Want to even let 'em in, they just want a spin. She, about her ends, got to play to win. Thinking back to back, like a double stack. If you can't handle that, you can step back. Working on her ends, clipping dead ends. Chasing men—could you picture that, fact. Like a runner back, not the quarterback. She can't get sake, so she lets 'em chase. Lead 'em on race, no need to rush watch her keep pace. Look 'em in the face while she makes 'em wait. Haters gonna hate, yeah, that's every day. She just laid out her plan, then execute it. She can't wait on you; she just has to move. You may say she chooses, but that's up to you. Playing by their rules, you were born to lose. Women gonna do what women gonna do. Men should do what men are supposed to do. Step up to the plate; this ain't first base. This is home plate; you should say your grace.

Mook

No time for the game with you.
This time, you going have to prove it to me.
Cause I been through the pain with you.
You could even say it's been hell with you.
Got me feeling shame with you.
Like I know I shouldn't even be with you.
Given all my time to you, trying to make it work with you.
Misting up the grind trying to lay with you.
I can't see clearly with you
I got cloudy mind with you.
Losing track of time with you.
Need to clear my mind.
Trying to focus on the paper, but you filling up my head.
Got me wondering if you lying to me.
Why you want to lay with me.
Why you want to call me babe.
Tell me what you want, I'm not into owing favors.
You just say you just want to do me favors, no need to repay 'em.
Tell my mind calm down, this is how you show me what you could
    ever tell me.
Really want to make it real, like how make me feel.
Like how you spell it, yep I promise I won't tell it.
Tell me, are you acting.
Tell me, are you playing.
I can't really tell is really real.
Are we really here? could this really be real.
This no fairy tale, we just made it through our hell.

Others could never understand how we stayed; yeah made it through
    the hell.
No more rainy days, only sunshine finds us in the shade, sipping
    lemonade.
Thankful for all the lonely nights, I found myself in pray.
Working on myself, found out I can do it myself.
I don't really need the help.
Tho I'm glad we made it with no shade, I got to say I'm thankful for
    the help.

Bre

This is s'um like new, and you have seen it true. Watching from a new frame, like, let me learn the game. She played the field just like a man, putting the boys to shame. The way she killed the game, man, she could have given you the game. Can't apply the pressure; I shouldn't even play this game. Time to learn the lesson; no time for second guessing. Take a chance, win or lose; you gotta make a move. Ain't no chess nor checkers; move with no point, like what I'm trying to prove. I like me; I like you, but the way you show, me I like me before you. I still like you; it's just me then you. I looked it up too; I come before you. How the alphabet does it, cold, flu, sick, let's be threw with this. Let's be true boys to men, this ain't the last dance. Can you have a chance? Do you have a chance? Clear the mind. Did you have a plan for approaching man? Got a plan or you working from the plan. Let's be clear: it's more than sex that comes with a chance. Romancing leads to healing, this sex, what a feeling. Making love come out—we all love sexual healing. Can this feel good for me? I want to stop; I can't see the danger in any future for me. I don't know what they are talking 'bout. The way that I see it, this is what they were all talking about.

Carren

This girl is really, some like of amazing. Even diamonds come with flaws; that's how GOD made 'em. Perfection is a curse 'cause they hate, babe, but haters got to hate so love 'em babe. A gift and a curse—let it motivate you. Remember who you are; they can't stop you, babe. Your love is never toxic; it brings growth, babe. Never get drained, like how you tell 'em keep it moving, babe. Focused on the grow; if they are not sorry, not sorry, but I gotta go, babe. Never play with the waiting; we want action, babe. What's the plan? Let me know, like why we are waiting. No movement is going stagnant; you have been contemplate lately. This is all you want, so you are really happy. You only live once. What do you really want? The gold and the fame, or no more rainy days. One without the other, I see pain coming. Pain with another is a joy, babe, but I don't want to hear we can make it, babe. I want to see the effort that has grown lately. Don't act silly, 'cause love ain't lazy, sure, strong, but I don't know 'bout patience.

Rain

At first glance, this one looks like a good girl. The true meaning of don't judge a book by its cover. Still, she's lovely and never seems to be lonely. Her love got game; she only knew how to give pain. Stand close, and it will turn into a ghost. Like when the wind comes and blows the bust, there's no rush, but she's used to saying that's all she wrote, folks. On to the next, like what you expect. Coasting through life with so much to choose, new dude like guest night, but nothing to prove. She seems crazy 'cause she ain't holding back, wild-side power ranger. This girl just transformed, the way she takes control makes you want to call it love. She never meant to give hope; she was only out for herself. I can't say I love you. Don't be down; no rainy days 'cause she has gone to another. She never said I loved you. Don't confuse the pleasures that she gave. She likes to say that she's a giver; have you dig the tune she is singing? She likes the attention, but she knows she sum like a vixen. Poison is in the veins, but the way she is acting, you would never know until it starts showing. Heart really cold, like it was never about growth. Hurt, 'cause she is not in a rush to be hurt by anything looking like love. To her, that sounds like being in bad joke.

Mama Knows

Looking back, we can see Mama was always right. Mama Knows everything that glitters ain't gold, and the same one you love will make you cry. Mama knows her baby can't stop 'em, if they want to go baby let them go. Yeah, it hurt you, but life goes on without 'em. Mama knows, baby, don't even try to fight if it's yours to fight for. Mama Knows life is like a box of chocolate; try two or three 'cause you never know what you could get. Mama Knows her words and her life don't mix; that's why Mama wishes she would've listened to her mama. Mama Knows where her baby could go; she wants you to put on a show and let the whole world see you grow. Mama Knows how her baby is feeling; they don't have to hear your feelings. Mama loves her baby and wants to have nobody hurt her baby's feelings. Mama Knows how to play the game, and only if she could give it to you would you have the game without so much pain. Mama Knows her baby has a chance; don't ever give up; Mama's always in your corner. At this point, you should know how Mama does it, she is the crew, and you don't want to see her come through. Ain't no ends to what Mama will do for her baby; that's some kind of love, baby.

Nikki

Here we go. This is someone you can take home to Ma. She knows just how to play the good girl and the classy lady. True, she nasty and likes the nasty he brings. When alone with her, there's no time to sleep, and a lot happens, but do you really want me to talk about it? We gave them what they want, it was loud with no talking. S'um Like make your mama proud and work what she gave you. Yeah, if she gave it, you got to work it. I like that. 😊 Give it here, and let's see how we work it. With the right perception, all the games we bring to an end. Play to win. Just who is the opponent? Let 'em know, cause I don't see no competition. Ready go, what happened to the opposition? They must have gotten disoriented. Moving like chess, it's no guess it's mate in three moves. Keep it nice. That's short and sweet like two goodbyes. Running through your mind is just a lie, these thoughts just want to die. Like spin the broke it's going to take more than one chop at this.

No head space; head all out of place. That's headless, like the head gave chase with no grace. Stand tall, no falling; keep yourself in place. Don't forget, life is akin to a race. It could be fun.

Alex

What do you think of this thing they call "love"? Is it not just the fools talk or the wise man plait? Wasn't it said, "For it is better to have loved then lost than to have never loved at all?" How great of a love must have been lost, for still, some loss is a lot more for the vain of love. Is this a chance of fate, or are we just tempting our faith? See, is it God's plan? For this pain or those choices that lead to this frame. Like all things, we love to play the blame game; only the strong win cause the weak give in. Is it not the same with love? For what sane person would, if tested, follow the examples of Romeo and Juliet? Sane being the key, then is love sane there for unsafe, like the same thang that'll make you smile will make you cry? How can love cause pain? Is it like why flowers don't grow without rain? Too much sunshine cosie pain, like the genius who calls out to OPP? But true love, real love, sounds like a dream. If I dare, how can I love you if I don't love myself first? So if I love myself, can I then love another without ending the love for myself? You can't love two people at the same time the same way, and that includes myself. So if I love another, I can't love myself. Thus I can't love another cause I can't love myself. So how do you love another, it's said by loving yourself. So if I love myself, I love others. If I'm happy with myself, I'm happy with others. No need to love another for their love, they have to love themselves, and I have to love myself. So when we love ourselves, we love one another.

Look at It

The way that it's done, I just want to look at it. Excuse the face; we just want to look at it. You won the race; I'm taking second so I can have a better look at it. Look at the curves; I might crash trying to look at them. No push to start; it's not automatic; it's a classic. Just look at it. Like birds, we have no plans, but still, it's you we're looking at. See the clouds; I'm daydreaming so it's you I'm looking at. Yep, that is what I want. Get mad and turn around so I can look at it. That's it right there; don't go anywhere; just let me look at it. I got the picture, but it's not the same as when I look at it. Bottom to top, bad or good, that's it, so let's have a look at it. I'm loving it and it's so cool you can't see it when you look at it. Don't try to come near; I'll have a look at it. No, these eyes don't dry; we want to look at them. Like ripe fruit to the sight, mouth waters and soul bowl when we look at it. Admittedly, we long for a taste, but the pleasures in the chase are where I can look at them.

Zena

Go ahead and send a pickle. If you wet it, make it purple. You know you want me to hurt you. No holding back; let me work with you. I like it when you twerk. Let me hit it like I'm trying to break in. I'm trying to get in; it feels like I have no end. Slip in; naw, that's not what's next; it doesn't fit in; you've got to work it in. Nothing like the rest; make you hold your chest. Who knows who's the best? Even though I've never failed a test, give it your best. I wouldn't dare say the best, but how do the others compare? Check the flow, stroke, then the growth, and how you feel it coming up slowly. Stop; you don't want to let me pass. I'm going too fast; you don't want to crash. I make you laugh, and I find your spot. I got you open, and you wanted me to take the shot. Now you're blushing and you're kitty's gushing. Boiling hot and needing for me to touch you, given pressure, reliving pressure. I can't have you second-guessing; you got to know I'm given pleasure. Just like the king, we are going to do it your way, whatever it takes, as long as we win. From your top to your bottom, then back to your top, I'm driving slowly over your hill and curve. I'm trying to take you in; give me a minute and let me observe.

Violet

She's the one who leaves them purple-hearted. Rather leave 'em dead, don't want the troubles of being depleted just for you to still wind up dead. She doesn't see how they figured, you among the living, and it feel like dragging the dead along with you. She'll shop it; another one gets cropped out of the picture. What's her plan? Don't worry, life starts and ends as a solo mission. In war, some go missing, regroup, redeploy, and finish the mission. MIA, leave the stray to the MPs. I see you enjoying a sunny Miami day. Like they say, work hard, play harder, and if she does it on her own, she can pay to play. She was smiling, keeping cool, and laughing like excuse me, sir, but do you see a ring or caller on her finger or neck? Playing as they give it their best guess. Oh, she keeps them on point; they don't want her to get violent. Play the slow jam as she fades them off in the background; make it a violin cover cause you know they cry under the cover. No minute, man, you got to be able to handle the fight she gave; not saying she wild, but you got to prove yourself to this stallion.

Helen

You say you will die for it; words were never true. Yet you believe you want it, so you call it true. When asked to prove it, we meet every excuse. Still, your shown faith, for only "I love you" is said. I must admit, I do not know what this looks like. You see when I see them saying, "I love you," and the things they do. I'm lifted, thinking I must be a fool to chase and crave this love of fools. Only the love of a fool has no end; you see, there's nothing in loving men. We all die, and everything comes to an end, still happiness is the end. Forever, mankind calls out to me to let my arrow fly and find the one that their eye desires. These selfless requests will one day be the reason why they lie and you cry. Should we peddle the child that's spoiled by getting all they want, and still they'll ask for more? Finding they meet Hurt and Pain, saying the stain on my arrow was laced with poison. A late reaction: now I'm the cause of their life's destruction; until more is wanted, then that was just a disruption. It could be your choices and not my happenings that lead to your distraction. We are all kind of focused, and can only hear lies. So Love is for nobody, and trauma is made for everybody.

Untitled

As I move, I find myself moving through the day. I've found it true as a day turns into two, and two into a week, and a week grows into a month, and a month becomes a year. So you'll find yourself in time, and anything worth having is worth the weight. Time heals all wombs even unto the dead, less they stay dead. Life gives pain, and pain gives growth. These are the gifts of time. Life's not all bad, and all Pain don't hurt. Leave Fate alone and embrace Wisdom. The greatest of the greatest fathered Choice and Chance. Time you see, give to all with the selflessness of nature. Only Time is both the Giver and Receiver, the Taker and Replacer. For you see, it came from Time that you first saw Hate; if you keep up too fast, you've lost them. Through Time, it all came to the worst of men and the best of men. Lest with Time, you don't meet Wisdom or Intuition, know all Change isn't Good. Time is just without cause; it births without thought. So Time made Good, but you could not know it. So Time made Learnings and you called it Bad. It's truest that Time made Good And Bad, but you yourselves made Lies and Truth. Yet Time brings Light, not so for Time came out of the Dark. All of these, then Time shall give Love.

Jackie

Tell me, how was your night? Was it the same as almost every other night? It's too long, but not long enough to get the job done. Why's it so hard to work for Dr. Heartbreak, with what seems to be the same lady coming over and over again with the same story? They can't learn what the doctor tells me; you see, we all want to be loved. Oh, the pain a mother endures to give birth to a child, and the way to heaven is graded by death how the doctor gives them joy. Brighter days with sunshine and shade—this heartbreak is just the foreshadowing of better days to come. Life goes on, and every day is a chance for a change, and every new day might bring growth. Dr. Heartbreak isn't selling drugs, even though they leave with the hope of love. You don't get it; the doctor told me people think love isn't supposed to hurt. They never think about the pain they are going to go through to find just one. Little is known to them about anyone's wants. Yet time and time again, they sing their song, how give, and they give, and it's never enough to make the love stand the test. We just do our best, and then what's to be said of the rest? The doctor will be in soon and get it off your chest.

Sum Special

Morning wood got me waking up all horny, so she peeks at me. I can't leave her lonely. We end at the same time by knocking on my wood, making her feel good about swimming in the ocean with no Marko. She cum for the pole, drinks the pole slow magic poison, goes down, slows too much touching, let me get some suction, babe. No rushing, I am. Have you been gusting in your favor? I'm tasting a non. I ain't lusting this could be cozier on planks; we are toasting our bodies in motion, and we like the end, but we just keep on going.

Ellá

This is every woman, known to man as GOD's greatest gift—that's women. Girl power, woman power—let's have a moment of silence for all these beautiful flowers. Every day, she blooms; even the fines of wines can't compare. She is the decadence that gives life to men's will. Not for the chase of gold, she is what was once told to men as little boys. For she holds the control for men to give up power and to seize power. She truly is the most dangerous of all the roses. Please take hedheed and watch your words, for soft words of love are their own kind of potent. Who said hell has no fear like a scorned woman? What a fall from grace. On earth, where is a more pulchritudinous place to be than the place she is? She is wu for wuing the tantalizing feat she poses for mere men. She is love, full of rations with untold amounts to give, worthy to receive—a goddess indeed. We see you, and thank you, all of you. From the beauty of the feminine mind to the depths of the curves and veins. How all of you come together in a magnificent garden-like twist.

Seuss

Shhh, and listen for a second and hear what he and she say. Give me a minute. You see, lay down with the dogs and come up with flees. Dogs are man's best friend, and all men are dogs, they say to me. Can't you see the dog just likes to bury the bone, then he's on his way home? These birds of the same feather are twerking and tweeting as they flock together. They eat; I see food. Mom, put this fish in a bucket. This big fish won't fry on a grill. King of the hill, come up my hill. Up a hill, down a hill just to kill time to you kick the bucket, or Jill for Jack going down the hill. Tell the end, remember kissing in a tree? How growth goes bittersweet the fruit of a mulberry bush, how this is the home of the finest weasels. The squirrel comes down to fetch a nut, and the widow spins her lonely webs, then lays down and waits for others to try. What perfect meaning to till death do us part? So the heartless is for the coldest; with you, I will meet the end. You say true love as if William wrote biographies and not tragedies. For how perfect is a sweet death—never to have known the loss of another and yet not to fear the loss of another or leaving another. This is not to be for someone who must go at times until the time for their departure. But it's still better to know what was had than to lose the memory of love.

Qabila

To be is not the question. But to be is all that is needed. Yes, true, we do eat, drink, and relieve ourselves. It seems that somewhere, we were fooled by these tricky words. Rat race, you see, now how much better are we than these animals we cage to watch or hear them eat? So we're civil, to what degree? For how many truly great men have you, the horde, slain? Note how they don't fight; they only ask that you look back at their work, for you know not what to do. Even when men do their best for the other, men find their best in trying to control man's nature. Can we still not live and let live? If I should say so myself, to each his own. For good is to evil, and evil is to good. Stop your teaching of rhetoric, or this could soon look like a false prophecy. And still, man cannot truly and fully enjoy the best life. For love has not a covenant with man. As if damned by God to chase and please until it's time to leave. Some seem to have it, but if only we could pop their hood and see what they really think. Would things get messy only if they had tech? Grandma wouldn't think Shade was cool, and the rude boy was bad. Yet to want your love from another 😆 if you love them is not how it works. If you need to have your love, you should first give it to yourself so you can then teach it to someone else. Man can do that, which can be tough if only the teachers could learn with the students. For who has the true answer to love?

Tina

Here's another one. From the outside, this could fool anyone. Everyone should wonder if it's possible to be raised by savages. At this point, even the slickest city-goer has to follow this rugged smooth Southern thang. Even a man with half a brain could figure out the boldest of things to come out of the South. Like a runaway slave, we got donuts, Vick and Pete blowing smoke out the freight train hatch. The world watches in wait to get aboard. Yes, it comes with that hospitality. You like greens, potatoes, and cornbread. All these things are rape and twice as nice as coming out of the kitchen. We have to say we like the smoke that shows it's hot. Let's start the fire and sleep under the stars tonight. Oh, my liberty, if given to me, my pleasure in you would I enjoy. Yet time and time have not brought us near. Paid in full, you still mistreat me. Is this not the act of a hoer? How I wish to see something that I might truly see. For this tale of Fally has only a till to follow.

Madea

You should know to be careful about what you wish for. You're not like God, and there's no hell like the vengeance of a woman scorned. Why so when it's not that it was done for your hurt? All things must grow, and the end of pain is death. So fear not, but be slow to judge, for how did you use love, and what else is there for you to gain? Was it not all part of your plan, or did you start with no end in mind? Oh, how the wild things grow! This would make for a great show. Imagine it starting with something along the lines of hello. Could you believe that with just a glance, I was taken in thought, the words I spoke aloud? I must be mistaken, for whom has seen love at first sight without finding still only nights? It's only no fun when you don't know the rules. Be cool; you can learn the rules. With one shot, he can be all into you and do things that you say prove he loves you. Still, he becomes a liar, a cheat, and a no-good heathen, only causing you to judge. What do you think while you deliberate? Maybe things didn't start out quite right, but what does? Maybe they think differently; they have a different take on love. Can any one person fight the words of a goddess and win? The craft of cunning is more treacherous than white water rapids. It's best not to resist; just enjoy the road. Every day is a new part of your journey, and every journey has its own lessons. So grow and learn from what can't kill you, and give your love while letting others give their love; sin your love hurts their love.

Irone

If I've failed to grasp your true love's hand by now, pardon the indiscretions of making love wait. However true, admittedly, the being of each state started off fun. Off to the next when things aren't fun. We want to stop the music and get another one soon with those moves. Stop, don't watch those clocks, you have to move them. There's a party you've been waiting to get to. Every time, it seems to last longer until the end of the song. With a promise of the ring, you open up to the promise of love without knowing the cost in pain. Shouldn't we know that this is a selfish game where all the best players hide their greed until their wedding day. Then would you say all that you need and express your greed. How could we get it when we know all that you need to be given? If only cupid shot had fail, dare I say that dreaded day. Let's not shoot the messenger for you; the master knows best at that. So before going to bat, I'm glad I got to bat. Home runs back to back like Homer's son; both teams have fun; just know that every father tells his son only one team can win. Just know I hope it's yours, son; that's why we say take one for the team. Yes, by any means, I want you to win. Still it's okay to have fun with the other team; just remember that losing is no fun. Just ask the daughter's sons of sons of sons, but never the father of a daughter.

Dasha

I finally get it, but it's clear to me you even did and might not be willing. Ah, tell me what you do for her that another man can't do even better; how about what you do for her that she can't do for herself? She cooked for you and her, and then those clothes you wore were the same clothes she washed. Boy, you need to stop that and start thinking. That's a dangerous man when he starts thinking. Either way, let's bet she stays; we all know how long she has been with him the long way. Ah, how long has she been waiting anyway? Day after day, up to today, from the first day. She is on day one, planning to play until the end, son. You still ain't put a ring on it. Understand that with your playing son, she'll end up lying next to another's son. Yeah, fun and games must be explained. Boys have fun, and girls learn games. In the long run, all boys are funny sons to them. Pop gun, BB gun, she likes it when you go get a real gun. Never right, because you ain't shooting anything but those kids out. Life lessons often turn out messy, with people trying to fix a mess. Instead of leaving people and life to fix themselves, as long as I did my part right.

Perdita

Tell me how many times you have loved, only to have found that lost again. Like the season, you should know love can be gone with the wind as if it were an autumn leaf. Take time to reflect on how every leaf was green and true to its color. Only through the change in season do they turn and die. It's not so funny how the dead leaves flesh the tree, but we people seem to not be able to leave the dead with the dead. The tree gives all, and we only have words to speak. The tree lost all, but the roots will remain. How much can you take? What was that feeling like to have lost? Tell the lost tree all about it on the paper I lost to you with the pineal you made from my core. Is it the same as if you gave it all in the hope of just getting more time? All of you, you gave; there was none left of you. Only the root in the dart, like a grave, shall remain. The pain of what you gave gives sight to what you lost. Like the tree who gave, words can do me no good. The things of need have been missed with, for all things have a time; as ashes to ashes, who you know love could be dead.

Temere

Has there ever been a woman who saw a man and took pause, not just in awe but for clarity. This is what I mean: you say my name with the faith that you will hypnotize him into your will. Let me say sorry, for it's not that it's fake love, just not his true love. See, you tell me what you want from a man without thinking about what kind of man is fit for you. The man you could captivate with, no need to plead with me, is the easiest for you. Thoughts of the best—the man that stands above the rest. You woman, stop and think. Are you truly the best choice for him too? Is it fit for him to do this or that and find that he still must change for only you. The unforeseen pain you plan to give that man who should be another's man. They do you wrong; they know just what you want, but what you want changes them. Watch how they stay the same time and time again. You both find pain; what must we do for love. No, somebody just for me who just wants me. That is you; just tell me, will it be the same for you? Will they be the one for you, and friends count too, or didn't you say I'm your friend and the only one that's needed. You will meet your equal if you want to be equal, but this plan for my arrow will only bring sorrow. Take the time you need, like the archer, and learn what the one you want needs before the pain begins.

Sorenson

Oh, tell me, what is it you think you truly desire? How shall we go about fulfilling every desire? Shall another be the cause to bring forth your desire, then will they find one doesn't deserve? Wildly, without thought, the arrow shall fall and pound him. With no way out or one way out, you'll never let the prayer escape. The cost of this again could be a pain, but how could the joy belong to another? How did the hunter become the hunted? If only you could hear the ghost in the halls of love, all would halt their pursuit and fill themselves before attempting to catch another. But in one ear, then out there, they never heard a word still in the rings that go around the rose tree. If you should find time, think, and rewind about the thrones, you find yourself unable to miss 'em. Living life a reckless and ruthless life, how many hearts found you to be the cause that led to their deaths? Who would have ever thought that love could bring this kind of pain with it? So I ask you: What is it worth to have a dream you can't live? I dare you to live a dream without the fear that this could be a nightmare. Can I truly say it'll be sweet in the end when you know all that glitter isn't gold. Just live your life and pray not for me to let the arrow of sorrow go, for life comes with its own pains. Let what is meant be if it's to be; then it will be when it's time to be.

Agon

It's a foot with no time to head to the races. Still, she'll get out the gate with one leg in front of the other. She's far from last, but first, who knows who's going to take it. Leave it on the field; it feels like a fight for life. How sweet, with an afterthought that my cake wasn't meant for me to taste. So tell me who wins when you're all lined up with cake. Take a break, go get a bite, enjoy the smell they make while they bake, and stop trying to break the bank. Shopping around makes it hard to stay with just one style. One day, love will show you the trick it plays on you. When everyone's a player, you have to hate the game. But still, you're played by the maker of the game you forgot. Gem for a gem, like a shield for a shield, let's lose our wets and make the fool's trade. I'll keep the apron and mitts to go with the heat of this mission. Well done, and one thousand and one ways to serve the Katt. Get full and phat before the game. It's an eating contest, and fear not, this love bullshit won't defile the body, but watch not to be the server. Still, be not judgmental, for the judges don't play; they spectate and say who to pay. How arrogant this game is that to play is to lose and to lose is to win. But only those who never play can say they never lose, except for myself.

Señora Mentecato

It's, or it's; either way it is clear you don't or didn't know the right way. Not the wrong way or the worst way, just your way. Maybe, like if your plane had wings you could fly. Sorry, you're, or yourself, is going down, down, down; dow-own babe. Does it feel like rain from the sky? A reminder of the stormy, lonely nights. Over and over, we try this long kiss goodbye. While thinking of those awful lies you tell. When I see who it is, let's hope not to find one another and let it be not another like you. Waking up to see WE have grown and how nightmares are only a cure while dreaming, how sweet it is to go to sleep. Counting sheep, singing lullabies, and hopes whisk you away with the sands. How it fails, the dream of the best man. When to win, you must be the last man, even when all men want to be the first man, if not the only man.

Vera

This isn't as simple as moving on to black and white. It wasn't just a waste of time. Every step was made with the end in mind. Just try and hide while I'll seek to win. This won't be the twin of last year as if I haven't trained in wait for this opponent. See, the plan is to play you, not the clock. Watch as they all think of winning without a path of stones. It seems so many go stray or get lost, never to be found. While those who take the hate and envy get closer to the goal. Go for it; WE say, "You run the track while WE play the field." Same team, singles spots, but you play against them. All cool, the team wins, but not cool how the team breaks up, and we can't be friends in the end because we both played to win. Tell the truth; you can trust me; sorry, I want to cut it, and that doesn't help us mend. Do tell me why you let a friend win when, if you're my friend, one would think you want to see me win. No, indeed, my friend. I want you to win, but only if it doesn't stop my win. The way it goes is that you can get another or have two queens, but one wrong step, the king is trapped. This could turn into a deadly match, a sprint to the first mate—what a fine game for a king who says checkmate.

She Say

She was saying dumb shit like she wished he was me. Because I'm the one, and she knows it, I'm bringing dah drip. I'm a hit den dip; I'm not trying to trip. Say what, cum again, go hang out with the Klix. Hit the side hoes and pass 'em to your bro. Yeah, I'm tripping, but I know she already knows. How? Because I don't hide or waste time on a lie. So when I hit, I make her say yeah, the world is mine. She and every woman in it. I'm sure she gets it. She is saying dumb shit like she blows my mind, enjoying spending time, like wasting time, still enjoying what she is getting, how time is gifted. Sorry, I can't see us doing it quicky; I like to get all in it like I'm trying to kill it or keep it.

Carlo

Should I try to see if I can put this together? We shall see if my handwork is as good as that of those skilled with a pin. Let us try and make the man of women's dreams. We must take our time while remembering they may not care about the process. Don't be slow in getting it, but moving too fast will lead to a crash. Just being mindful isn't going to cut it, and if plans are to make a man, well, they just cut them. Start over; maybe we should try to start with seeing if it will be able to see. Foolish, why would we start with the thing that will lead the man astray? True, he does not yet have the mind to differ from illusion and fantasy. Should we seek a model to reference, and then maybe we will know just where to begin? Are there any men who cannot pass the test? Christ should be the best, but wait close to his chest; he holds chastity next to his breast. Socrates, please, would say he's only better than other men, knowing that he's no better than any other man. Well, where can we find this dream where the lovers never had to skim? Just look at how plotting helped Romeo and Juliet. If only 😩, we could make all men AND women with noise that grew when they told a lie. Yeah, but we know nobody wants that like; who knows the right answer to IS IT BIG?

Faith

Should this even be the case with having the same mother and father, these sisters truly forging an even deeper bond? Their parents are reminded that it was they themselves who taught them to share. But not like this. Young man, could you please play fair? Is it not fair that the rules state that all's fair in a war of love? These sisters are allied with each other to be the rest of what they believe to be the best. In this family, there's no fighting, and from the least to the best, everyone gets a chance to go. I want that. Don't say that. What's that? Don't ask that. You like that. We want to answer that. You want to try that. You do not like that. I'm with that for you. If that were for me, you would've never asked that. So we're going to try that. Give me time to learn about the trouble that comes with that. Why wait? Are you cool like that? Just not with my sister like that. Oh, you are going to maybe hit her with a bat. It could be something like that. So what are you saying about that? Maybe my friend and I might be cool like that. Maybe you are not cool like that. I'm cool, and this coco hit like that. Cool, break the rules, and the three sisters don't fight about that. The girls are fools; that's what their hating fathers say to them. Fools don't get the rules and lose; their mama told them how to get what they want. So a third is better than a whole when the third comes from that, which is ten times bigger.

LEYMAH

Let's make this big and bold and just as bad as a brick house. If you truly want it, then you have to go all out. Don't back down; show 'em what you're all about; now go show out. As if big mama in the house; ain't nobody bought to fight, we ain't trying to get put out. See, I knew they could act right. Now that everyone is in their assigned places remember your role. There's to be no more chasing; we're just setting plates, and don't think we're just waiting. Please, thanks, and I appreciate the GOOD LORD has given, but this ain't no waiting mission. As if I could hear GOD saying, go get it. You can sit and listen, or just don't show up like a missed period when you mist up. You listen, but you still want to get it. It's like that thing when trying to find it, but only gets hard to find; only when you're not trying to find it, to the point you'd overlook it, does it allow itself to be found. Let's admit it: we don't know how to find this thing we all seek. If that is the truth, then have we found common ground? While on these grounds, as holy as we wish them to be, we dare not compromise, but let us see what else could arise. If there's no way to agree without a dispute, then let that be our way, and there can be no way, you go your way and I'll go mine. For you see, this world is round, so all things are bound to meet. Why do all those we consider great only seem to want to achieve peace with whatever they are to meet?

Felisha

Choosing to win or lose. Something some people never even give a thought to. They must be like you, even though there's only one of you. As many fish as there are in the sea, how many could equal you? The pick of every man to have at his side, knowing that you bring fortune upon the grace of your women. But as fast as they can win, the wind at some point comes to an end. Only fools choose to fall in love, spanking into a debtors pit. Still, all into the last chip, saying lady lucky, pick me up from this dip. Too late it will be, you see, cause plays for keep, unlike you. She saw you as weak and unworthy to keep, and you, yourself, chose not to keep her. And before you lose, and tell her bye. Before you have a chance to try, she silently says bye as she waves like a theft in the night. Leaving you with no way to think of a win again. A muse in disguise, even if you try to hide. Few take note of your flaws and head straight for your fall. As clumsy as you are, how could you lead so many to think you were lucky? Thinking they had stumbled upon a charm when you stumbled into them. In the end, they are sure to see how wrong they are, and to themselves, they shall declare themselves to be the foolish ones. I wish that if time went back, they would take back their warm embrace and the words that took them up in passion.

Psyche

As we take a moment in time, with what is called hindsight twenty-twenty nowadays. Maybe we will see what was foretold to come. It's as if it's by some god's design for you to feud with the mother of your lover. I hide my love in the dark as if I'm a demand serpent. How this was planned to fail the moment I set my sights on it was I who missed and turned myself into my target. Foolish me has escaped me, unbound and free to run wild. Oh, what deceit the bow and arrow shell burned to me. If only you could be true and not change your word, as if they were children who don't change but grow. Knowing how my tail ends let me enjoy the little time that was well spent. I've seen time and time again that the odds of fate play the worst way for the souls that these arrows take. It was daring of me to try and save the one who took my sight. I'm trying to sway things to go my way with hard work and effort. And in just one night, with the loss of faith, the pendulum broke away from what I was trying to bend. What was equal now has been uncovered as deceitful, but it's not me I was trying to hide. In the eyes of the gods, mankind is amusingly distasteful, but we still love to watch you try. The life you have been given is the greatest quest. But the greatest test is to overcome your best by doing better on the next test. Seeing fate had put you against what you think is best, I must lay you to rest, for there are rules that must be upheld. Myths aren't fairy tales, and with a drink of ambrosia, I shall only have pleasure without the soul. My truths have been told, and my beloved is gone.

About the Author

Who could know a person better than their mother? So as she said, "My baby just in love with love." Still, as I grow, I can't seem to find a better high, than the one newly discovered love gives. Yet truly, the world taught me hard lessons in giving and receiving love. So I ask myself: is it better to give or receive? Should I love another as I love myself? I've always wanted love, but to win it as a prize, I'd be led to lay schemes. So I say who would do those deeds desired by the one they love, knowing that that person or anyone else would never do anything to repay your kindness. Give without expecting anything in return, not even a thank you, which we all deserve. Even as a child, I was able to think yes, sir, no, sir, yes, ma'am, no, ma'am, please and thank you, and wow, I was able to get away with a lot. Because all people are humans and want respect.